animal countdown

laura vaccaro seeger

NEAL PORTER BOOKS

HOLIDAY HOUSE / NEW YORK

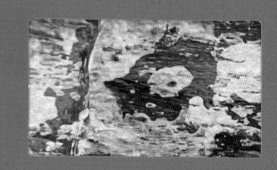

nine

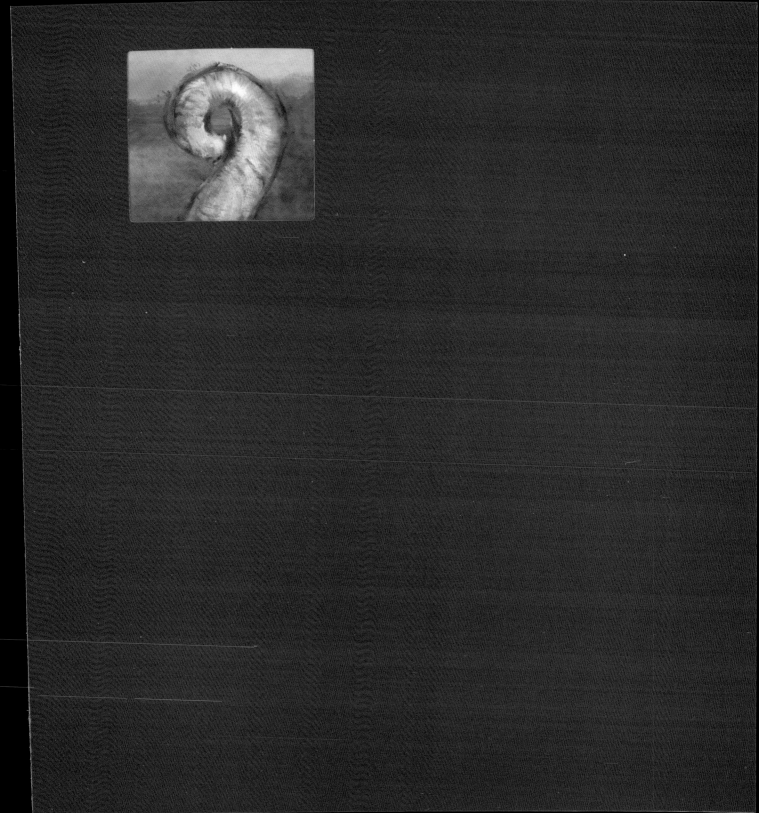

eight

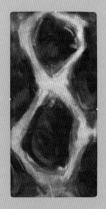

seven

six

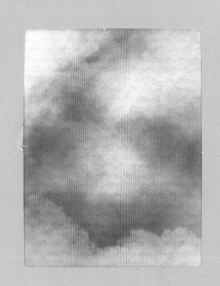

five

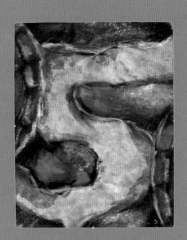

four

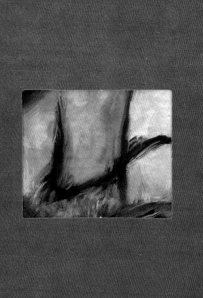

three

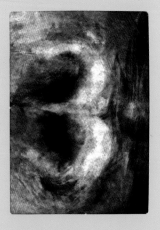

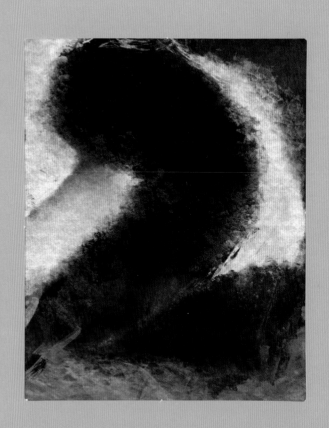

**All of the animals in this book
are threatened or endangered, some critically,
due to exploitation, pollution, vulnerable habitats,
and climate change.**

SEA OTTERS

Where are they from? Sea otters are native to the North Pacific Ocean.

What are they like? They weigh 50–70 pounds and have a lifespan of 10–20 years.

What do scientists call them? A group is called a raft, like a boat. The young are pups.

How do they live? Sea otters spend most of their waking hours looking for food, 9–12 hours every day! But this is time well spent—they help to keep kelp forests alive by eating sea urchins and other kelp-eating creatures.

What are they threatened by? Sharks, pollution, hunting, oil spills, and food scarcity.

ELEPHANTS

Where are they from? Elephants are native to the forest, savannas, and deserts of Africa and Asia.

What are they like? They weigh up to 9 tons, and are the largest land mammals, consuming 300 pounds of vegetarian diet per day, with a lifespan of 50–70 years.

What do scientists call them? A group is called a herd. The young are calves.

How do they live? Elephants are matriarchal animals—that means their herds are led by females—and they are highly intelligent and very social. They create forest clearings allowing plant growth and sustenance for smaller animals.

What are they threatened by? Habitat loss, hunting, and human conflict.

GIRAFFES

Where are they from? Giraffes are native to the savannas of Africa.

What are they like? They grow 14–18 feet tall and are the tallest animals on Earth, with a lifespan of about 26 years.

What do scientists call them? A group is called a herd. The young are calves.

How do they live? Giraffes are intelligent, quiet, long-necked animals. They primarily eat leaves and twigs that cannot be reached by other animals, promoting growth and providing open areas for smaller wildlife to thrive.

What are they threatened by? Habitat loss and disease.

DOLPHINS

Where are they from? Dolphins are found all over the world in oceans and fresh water.

What are they like? They weigh up to 1,400 pounds with a lifespan of 40–90 years.

What do scientists call them? A group is called a pod. The young are calves who stay close to their mother for several years.

How do they live? Dolphins are highly intelligent marine mammals that help maintain and regulate the fish population for a healthy ecosystem.

What are they threatened by? Pollution, habitat loss, climate change, and fishing.

WHOOPING CRANES

Where are they from? Whooping cranes are native to North American wetlands, marshes, and fields.

What are they like? They grow to 5 feet tall with a lifespan of 25–30 years.

What do scientists call them? A group of whooping cranes is called a sedge. A baby whooping crane is called a colt.

How do they live? Whooping cranes are among the rarest birds. They travel in small flocks and eat amphibians, crustaceans, reptiles, and insects, and they provide food for foxes, wolves, raccoons, and other animals.

What are they threatened by? Hunting and habitat loss.

SEA TURTLES

Where are they from? Sea turtles have traveled the Earth's seas, bays, and lagoons for 100 million years.

What are they like? They weigh up to 1,100 pounds! And they have a lifespan of 50–100 years.

What do scientists call them? A group of sea turtles is called a bale, and a baby sea turtle is called a hatchling.

How do they live? Sea turtles are reptiles that nest on beaches, and they help maintain the health of coral reefs and seagrass essential to the survival of fish and crustaceans.

What are they threatened by? Pollution, poaching, habitat destruction, and climate change.

TIGERS

Where are they from? Tigers live in the forests, grasslands, and savannas of Asia.

What are they like? An adult male can weigh anywhere from 200–600 pounds! Tigers have a lifespan of between 15–25 years.

What do scientists call them? A group of tigers is called an ambush, and the young are cubs.

How do they live? Tigers are the largest wildcats. They love to swim and are afraid of fire. By preying on herbivores, tigers help to preserve the ecosystem by controlling overgrazing.

What are they threatened by? Hunting and habitat destruction.

GORILLAS

Where are they from? Gorillas live primarily in the rainforests of Africa.

What are they like? They grow to 6 feet tall and weigh up to 500 pounds with a lifespan of 40 years.

What do scientists call them? Family groups are called troops or bands, and babies are called infants. Just like humans!

How do they live? Gorillas are highly intelligent, calm, social animals. They eat leaves, twigs, and insects, and are helpful to the environment by dispersing seeds throughout the forest.

What are they threatened by? Habitat loss, poaching, and disease.

PANDA BEARS

Where are they from? Panda bears live in the mountain forests of China.

What are they like? They weigh up to 250 pounds, spend 10–15 hours per day eating, and consume a mostly vegetarian diet. They have a lifespan of 20 years.

What do scientists call them? A group of panda bears is called a cupboard or bamboo; the young are cubs.

How do they live? Panda bears like to climb and swim, and they don't hibernate. They help to keep the forest healthy by spreading seeds through their droppings.

What are they threatened by? A poor diet, poaching, and loss of habitat.

SNOW LEOPARDS

Where are they from? Snow leopards live in the cold high-altitude mountains of Asia. **What are they like?** They weigh up to 120 pounds and have a lifespan of 10–12 years. **What do scientists call them?** Snow leopards live together so infrequently that there is actually no term for a group of snow leopards! A baby is called a cub. **How do they live?** Snow leopards are shy, elegant, solitary animals. Their main prey are sheep, goats, birds, rodents, and other animals. Eating these animals helps preserve ecological balance. **What are they threatened by?** Habitat loss, poaching, decline in prey, and climate change.

Further Reading

Bar, Catherine and Anne Wilson. *Red Alert! Endangered Animals Around the World.* Watertown: Charlesbridge, 2018.

Clinton, Chelsea and Gianna Marino. *Don't Let Them Disappear: 12 Endangered Species Across the Globe.* New York: Philomel Books, 2019.

Gibbons, Gail. *Giant Pandas.* New York: Holiday House, 2021.

Munro, Roxie. *A Day in the Life of the Desert: 6 Desert Habitats, 108 Species, and How to Save Them.* New York: Holiday House Books, 2023.

National Geographic Kids' Mission Animal Rescue series

For Chris

Neal Porter Books

Text and illustrations copyright © 2024 by Laura Vaccaro Seeger
All Rights Reserved
HOLIDAY HOUSE is registered in the U.S. Patent and Trademark Office.
Printed and bound in June 2024 at Toppan Leefung, Dongguan, China.
The artwork for this book was created using mixed media.
Book design by Laura Vaccaro Seeger
www.holidayhouse.com
First Edition
1 3 5 7 9 10 8 6 4 2

Library of Congress Cataloging-in-Publication Data is available.

ISBN: 978-0-8234-4867-8 (hardcover)